Fact Finders®

DISGUSTING HISTORY

GRITTY, STINKY ANCIENT EGYPT

THE DISGUSTING DETAILS ABOUT LIFE IN ANCIENT EGYPT

WITHDRAWN

by James A. Corrick

Consultant:
Jen Houser Wegner, PhD
Associate Curator
Egyptian Section, Penn Museum
Philadelphia, Pennsylvania

CAPSTONE PRESS
a capstone imprint

Fact Finder Books are published by Capstone Press,
151 Good Counsel Drive, P.O. Box 669, Mankato, Minnesota 56002.
www.capstonepub.com

Books published by Capstone Press are manufactured with paper
containing at least 10 percent post-consumer waste.

Library of Congress Cataloging-in-Publication Data
Corrick, James A.
 Gritty, stinky ancient Egypt: the disgusting details about life in ancient Egypt / by James A. Corrick.
  p. cm. — (Fact finders. Disgusting history)
 Includes bibliographical references and index.
 Summary: "Describes disgusting details about daily life in ancient Egypt, including housing,
food, and sanitation"—Provided by publisher.
 ISBN 978-1-4296-5406-7 (library binding)
 1. Egypt—Social life and customs—To 332 B.C.—Juvenile literature.
 2. Egypt—Civilization—To 332 B.C.—Juvenile literature. I. Title. II. Series.

DT61.C594 2011
932—dc22   2010040799

Editorial Credits
Mari Bolte, editor; Gene Bentdahl, series designer; Svetlana Zhurkin, media researcher;
Eric Manske, production specialist

Photo Credits
Alamy: North Wind Picture Archives, 28–29, Paris Pierce, 25; Art Resource, N.Y.: The Trustees of the British
Museum, 16, Werner Forman, 23; Artville, 18 (left); The Bridgeman Art Library: Egyptian National Museum,
Cairo, Egypt, 27 (top), Index, Barcelona, Spain, 6–7, National Geographic Image Collection, cover, 10–11, 17,
Private Collection/Look and Learn, 21, 24; Corbis/Royalty-free, 4 (middle); Getty Images: The Bridgeman Art
Library, 9 (top front), De Agostini/G. Dagli Orti, 18–19; iStockphoto: ELENart, 4 (btm left), Goran Bogicevic,
4 (top left), Vladimir Korostyshevskiy, 4 (btm right); Library of Congress, 5 (btm right); Mary Evans Picture
Library: 12–13, Illustrated London News, 14–15; Shutterstock: akva, 9 (back), 27 (btm), freelanceartist, grunge
design, kmiragaya, 5 (btm left), Turi Tamas, fact box design element

Primary source bibliography
Page 9—from *Ancient Near Eastern Texts Relating to the Old Testament*, edited by James B. Pritchard (Princeton, N.J.:
Princeton University Press, 1955) and reprinted in *Everyday Life in Ancient Egypt* by
Lionel Casson (Baltimore: Johns Hopkins University Press, 2001).
Page 27—from *Ancient Records of Egypt; Historical Documents from the Earliest Times to the Persian Conquest, collected,
edited, and translated, with commentary by James Henry Breasted.* Chicago: The University of Chicago Press, 1906-07).

Printed in the United States of America in Stevens Point, Wisconsin.
092010   005934WZS11

TABLE OF CONTENTS

ANCIENT EGYPT
3100–30 BC

PAGE 9

3100–2700 BC
Narmer unites Upper and Lower Egypt. Memphis is the capital. Writing in the form of hieroglyphs appears.

2625 BC
The Old Kingdom begins.

PAGE 7

2589–2566 BC
Pharaoh Khufu rules and builds the Great Pyramid at Giza.

2181 BC
The Old Kingdom ends.

2055 BC
The Middle Kingdom begins. Its capital is Thebes.

1650 BC
The Middle Kingdom comes to an end.

PAGE 26

1650–1550 BC
Hyksos invaders conquer and rule much of Egypt. They bring the chariot to Egypt.

1550 BC
The New Kingdom begins.

1279–1213 BC
Pharaoh Ramses II rules Egypt.

THE GREAT PYRAMID BY THE NUMBERS

57,000,000 TONS (51,710,000 METRIC TONS)—total weight

23,000,000—approximate number of blocks

2.5 TONS (2.3 METRIC TONS)—average weight of one block

15 TONS (13.6 METRIC TONS)—weight of the largest block

756 FEET (230 METERS)—length of the pyramid's base on one side

13.1 ACRES (5.3 HECTARES)—total area of the pyramid's base

481.3 FEET (146.7 METERS)—the pyramid's original height

MILLIONS OF MUMMIES

It has been estimated that more than 70 million mummies were made during the time of the pharaohs.

MEDITERRANEAN SEA

THE CAPITAL
The capital of Egypt has changed many times. Thebes has been the capital four different times. Cairo was not chosen until AD 969.

LOWER EGYPT

NILE DELTA

GIZA
CAIRO
MEMPHIS

EGYPT

NILE RIVER

LEGEND

— RIVERS
▢ VALLEY OF THE KINGS
☆ CAPITAL CITY
● CITY

0   100 MI.
0   161 KM

N
W   E
S

VALLEY
OF THE
KINGS   ▢ ☆ THEBES

RED SEA

UPPER EGYPT

1069 BC
The New Kingdom comes to an end.

332 BC
Alexander the Great conquers Egypt.

305 BC
The Greek Ptolemaic family becomes Egypt's rulers.

30 BC
Queen Cleopatra VII dies. Rome conquers Egypt.

ANCIENT HISTORY

Ancient Egypt is known for its pyramids, pharaohs, and, of course, mummies! But it was also a place where backbreaking labor, deadly illnesses, and dirty rivers were common. For about 3,000 years, ancient Egyptians toiled under the hot sun. Pyramids had to be built. Mummies had to be made. And sand from the Sahara desert got in everything.

Ancient Egyptians lived along the banks of the Nile River. The river waters were polluted with human and animal waste.

Dangerous animals called the river home too. Hungry crocodiles lived along the river's banks, waiting for an unsuspecting person or animal to get too close.

During the flooding season, no farming could be done. Instead, the pharaoh required men to build the pyramids. They were not paid. Their work was seen as a service to the pharaoh and his family. Men worked for eight days and then rested for the next two days. Sometimes they were given free days for holidays. Other times they were given time off to work on their own tombs. Leaders liked to keep the peasants busy year-round. They thought that if their subjects were working, there would be less time for boredom and making trouble.

Nearly 70 pyramids were built around Cairo.

THE WORKING CLASSES

Who's the boss? In ancient Egypt, it was the pharaoh. Most pharaohs were men, but a few were women. The pharaoh was believed to be the earthly form of Horus, the Egyptian sky god.

After the pharaoh and his family, Egyptian society had three main classes. At the top were the rich nobles, who included governors and priests. They held most of the land and wealth. Below them were the artists and educated men. This class included doctors, lawyers, teachers, and recordkeepers called scribes.

The lowest part of society was the working class. More than 80 percent of the population belonged to the working class. Peasant men worked on farms and in quarries and mines. Women served as dancers, maids, or hairdressers.

After the yearly flood, it was the peasants' job to plow, plant, and harvest the fields. Some peasants had animals to pull their plows, but others had to do it themselves. Preparing fields and harvesting crops was backbreaking work. And a portion of every harvest went directly to the pharaoh as taxes.

Scribes held a high rank in ancient Egypt.

The Written Word

Be a scribe. More effective is a book than a decorated tombstone … A man is perished, his corpse is dust, all his relatives are come to the ground—(but) it is writing that makes him remembered.

From a writing exercise for apprentices wishing to become scribes.

Some work gangs chipped away in the quarries. Rock from the quarry was used to build the pyramids and other large buildings. Blocks of stone were cut by hand from the quarry floor and walls. These blocks weighed several tons each. The work was slow. The laborers' tools were made from stone or metals such as copper and bronze. Their tools dulled quickly. The soft blades chipped off only very small pieces of rock at a time.

Sometimes workers had to crawl under a stone to free it from the quarry rock. They wiggled into a space only slightly larger than their bodies. Their only light came from a small oil lamp. The workers breathed in stone dust that damaged their lungs. And there was always the danger of being crushed by the huge blocks.

Ships carried the stone blocks up or down the Nile. From the ship, large gangs of men used ropes to drag the blocks to the building site. It was hard, sweaty work under the hot Egyptian sun.

Working in the mines was even worse. Workers lay on their stomachs in tight-fitting tunnels and chipped out gold and gems. There was always the danger of being buried alive in a cave-in.

a section of the *Book of the Dead*

MAKING A MUMMY

For ancient Egyptians, death was a new beginning. Ancient Egyptians believed in the afterlife. People who died met Osiris, the god of the underworld. Those who passed the god's judgment lived forever. The dead were buried with religious texts and magical spells like those found in the *Book of the Dead*. The spells helped the dead make a successful passage into the afterlife.

The Egyptians believed that the soul of the dead returned to the physical body from time to time. The body could not be left to rot, or the soul might not recognize it.

Special workers preserved the body through a process called **mummification**. They started by removing the dead person's brain. First a metal hook was pushed up the body's nose and wiggled around to break up the brain. The brain would drain out while the rest of the body dried. Ancient Egyptians didn't know that the brain was important. To them, the heart was the most important internal organ.

mummification: the process of making a mummy to preserve a dead person's body

Next, they cleaned out the inside of the body. Workers removed the intestines, liver, stomach, and lungs. But they left the heart. Ancient Egyptians believed that the heart was used during the soul's final judgement.

The body was washed with water, then with palm wine. They packed and covered the body with a natural mineral salt called natron. The body was left to dry in the salt for about 40 days. Bodies were placed on slightly slanted tables to allow the fluids to drain.

FOUL FACT

Between the 1400s and 1700s, Europeans used mummies as a cure-all medicine. The bodies were ground into powder or mixed with other ingredients and eaten.

After 40 days, the natron was removed. The body was much lighter. Packing was sometimes stuffed inside the body to make it appear fuller and more lifelike. Finally, the body was washed with perfumed oils and wrapped with **linen** bandages. **Amulets** for protection were placed in the wrappings.

The mummy was then placed in a tomb. During the Old Kingdom, pharaohs' tombs were pyramids. The largest pyramids were at Giza. Later pharaohs preferred hidden underground tombs. Many of these tombs were in the Valley of the Kings.

Coffins were decorated to look like the person who had died.

linen: a cloth made from the flax plant
amulet: a small charm believed to protect the wearer from harm

BREAD AND BAD TEETH

Both rich and poor Egyptians ate a lot of bread. But theirs didn't come presliced from the grocery store. And it could be crunchy! Eating bread in ancient Egypt might mean losing a tooth.

Grain, such as wheat and barley, was the main food product of ancient Egyptian farms. The farms grew so much grain that bread and porridge were the main meals of farmers and laborers. Workers were often paid in grain or loaves of bread.

Bread was made into many different shapes. Sometimes the dough was shaped into tall cones. Other times, the dough was made into flat disks. Loaves shaped like fish or people have also been found.

Ancient Egyptians liked variety. They flavored their bread with spices or honey. Ingredients like dates, eggs, butter, and oil added some variety to the bread as well.

BREAD, CIRCA 1500 BC

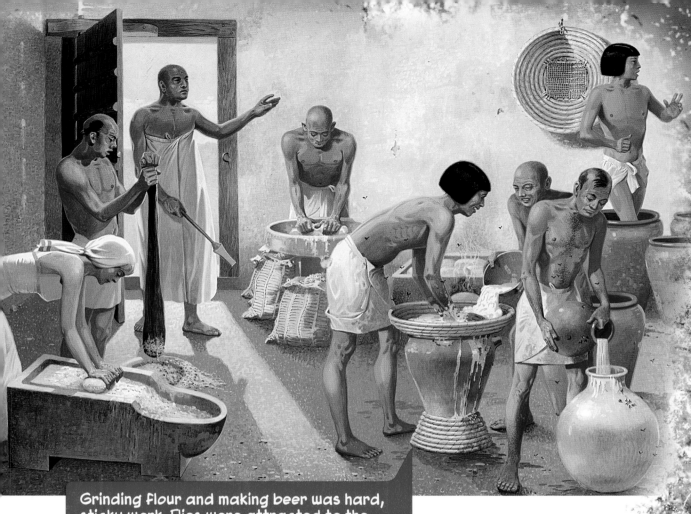

Grinding flour and making beer was hard, sticky work. Flies were attracted to the sweaty bodies and sweet beer.

Egyptian bread gave a new meaning to whole grain. Sand from the Sahara desert was everywhere. The sand ended up mixed into the bread flour. The gritty sand was rough on the teeth. Over the years, the sand wore the teeth down and exposed the **nerves**. People with damaged teeth found eating and drinking difficult and painful.

nerve: a thin fiber that carries messages of feeling from the body to the brain

Ancient Egyptians also ate a lot of fruit and vegetables. The rich soil by the Nile River made it easy for farmers to grow plenty to eat. Onions and garlic were particular favorites. Meals were washed down with beer and sometimes wine.

Fish and birds that lived in and near the Nile were also part of the standard diet. Other meats were expensive and eaten mostly by the rich. Ancient Egyptians had no way of refrigerating meat. They had to eat fresh meat quickly or it would spoil. They sometimes preserved meat by drying, smoking, or salting it.

No part of the animal went to waste. People ate the ears, brains, hooves, and guts. The blood was then boiled and used as a seasoning. Blood was sometimes left to thicken, roasted, and eaten as a pudding.

ONIONS

KEEPING CLEAN

Ancient Egyptians led short lives compared to people today. Many Egyptians died before they reached age 40. Illness was common. Many women died in childbirth. Injuries also made life risky. Even a small cut or a case of diarrhea could be deadly.

People in ancient Egypt didn't know about sanitation. Poor disposal of garbage and bodily waste caused most problems. Garbage piled up outside houses and in alleys. Flies and other disease-carrying creatures flocked to these areas. The ancient Egyptians did not have sewer systems to carry away waste. Instead they tossed their waste into the Nile and its **canals**. They used this same water for drinking and bathing.

Do you smell that? Then it's time for a bath. Egyptians bathed often, but they did not have soap. Instead, they used natron, the same stuff that was used on mummies.

The rich had bathing areas in their houses. The homes of the rich had as many as 10 rooms, so they had space to put in a bathroom. They bathed in bathrooms with tiled floors and painted walls. But poor people only had one-room houses made of mud bricks. They bathed in canal or river water.

canal: a channel dug across land to connect two bodies of water

Bathing in the Nile was dangerous and not just because of crocodiles. Tiny pests were always present. People who worked near the water, such as fishermen or brick-makers, were especially at risk to the creepy-crawlies. For example, a creature called the guinea worm entered the human body. It lived under the skin and could grow as long as 3 feet (0.9 meters). It caused painful blisters and infection.

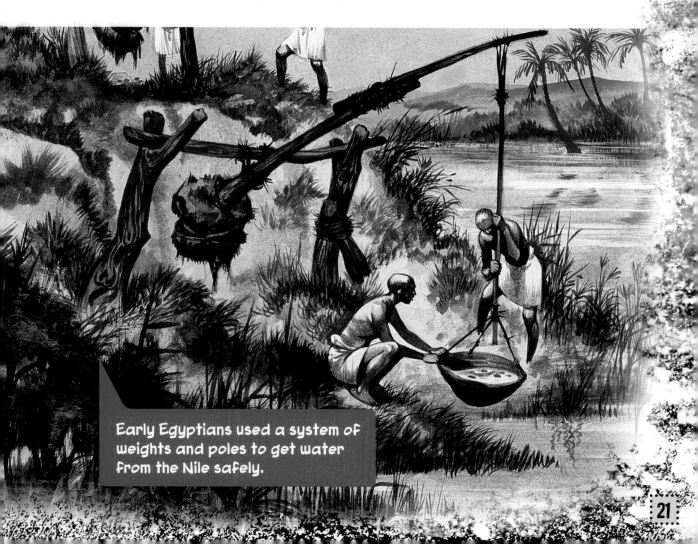

Early Egyptians used a system of weights and poles to get water from the Nile safely.

Lice were also a problem. Lice can carry disease. They lay their eggs in human hair. Men and women shaved their heads and bodies to rid themselves of lice.

Of course, this doesn't mean that the ancient Egyptians didn't care about hair. In fact, a head of thick, black hair was seen as a sign of youth. Like today, women with thinning hair got hair extensions, wigs, or tried various recipes to cure baldness. Some recipes included ingredients such as ox blood or donkey liver.

Rich people wore wigs to replace their missing head hair. The wigs were made of human hair, sheep's wool, or plant fibers.

Got something in your eye? The constantly blowing sand, glaring sun, and swarms of flies caused many eye infections. There were many blind and near-blind people.

The desert sand did more than hurt the eyes. People breathed the sand in, causing lung infections and other breathing problems.

FOUL FACT

One recipe for hair tonic called for mixing fats from animals like lions, snakes, and hippos. The mixture was then rubbed into the scalp.

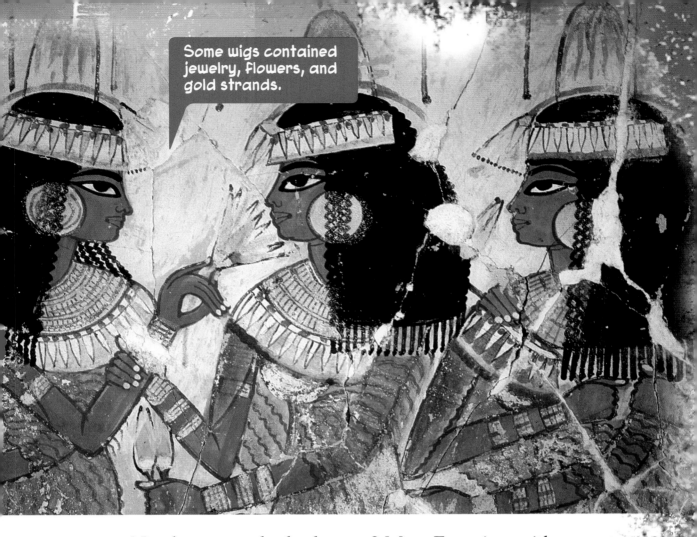

Some wigs contained jewelry, flowers, and gold strands.

Need to go to the bathroom? Most Egyptians either relieved themselves outside or into pots. But some rich people had toilets. These toilets had a stone or wooden seat with a hole in it. Below was a pot that sometimes contained sand. Just like a cat with a litter box, the user would cover the waste with sand. Of course, these pots had to be emptied. And their contents went the same place as everything else—into the river.

MEDICAL TREATMENTS

Need a doctor? You've come to the right place. Ancient Egyptians had some of the most advanced medicine of their time. But they still had some methods we would find gross today.

There were no medical schools, so older doctors trained younger doctors. There were many books that described illnesses and injuries in great detail. The books told the reader what to do in each case and whether something was curable or not. With this information, doctors could give medicines, set broken bones, and treat wounds.

Doctors in ancient Egypt could treat a variety of illnesses.

Doctors gave patients medicines made from strange or exotic ingredients.

Many ancient Egyptian cures were practical. For crocodile bites, a doctor sewed up the wound. Many medicines called for honey, which is a natural **bacteria** killer.

Other treatments depended on odd medicines and practices, and even magic. Some medicines contained animal waste, urine, or blood. One cure called for the patient to sip a special drink made from onion, honey, water, and a mouse's tail. Another remedy called for a mixture of grease and crushed ostrich egg. To try and cure blindness, a doctor would grind up two dry pig's eyes and mix them with honey. He then poured this mixture into the patient's ear.

bacteria: microscopic living things

SOLDIERING FOR THE PHARAOH

For most of its history, ancient Egypt did not have a professional army. In times of war, the pharaoh commanded the army. He **drafted** men as soldiers. Egyptians dreaded going off to war. Being killed and buried away from their homeland was something they feared.

Most ancient Egyptian troops were known as foot soldiers. They carried spears, axes, and heavy clubs called maces. Long-distance weapons were important too. Archers could attack from a long distance without much danger to themselves. Chariots allowed soldiers to fight without getting tired.

Ancient Egyptian soldiers did not have much protection from enemy weapons. They carried shields, but they were made of leather, not metal. The average soldier did not wear armor or a helmet.

Battle wounds were often nasty. A blow with an ax or a mace could cut or smash through bone. An ax could also cut deep into arms and legs or even take off a limb. Arrows could cut through an eye into the brain. A stone from a sling often crushed a skull or caved-in a chest.

draft: the selection of young men to serve in the army

Pharaohs were buried with models of soldiers. The models represented real soldiers and were meant to protect the pharaoh in the afterlife.

Prisoners of War

Slaves in ancient Egypt were often prisoners captured during battles. This ancient text describes prisoners of war in Egypt during the reign of Ramesses III.

I gave to them captains of archers, and chief men of the tribes, branded and made into slaves, impressed with my name; their wives and their children were made likewise.

Papyrus Harris, New Kingdom

DOING TIME

Thinking of breaking the law? Think again. The ancient Egyptians did not have a set of written laws. Instead pharaohs were in charge. Their word was law.

Ancient Egypt did have courts. Most trials were held in local courts. Some trials were held before a royal court. The pharaoh or his chief advisor was the judge.

Trials could be harsh affairs. Judges might believe that one side was lying. To get the truth, the judges had these people beaten with sticks.

Ancient Egypt did not have jails. Instead, criminals would have to pay fines or receive harsh punishments. A common punishment was 100 blows with a stick. Ears and noses might be cut off. Sometimes whole families could be punished for the actions of one member.

Murder and treason were punished with death. Execution methods included being burned alive, being run through with a wooden stake, and being eaten by crocodiles.

The royal court tried cases involving the death penalty.

Illness, injury, and hard work were only a few things that shaped how ancient Egyptians lived. They had a lot to worry about, both in this life and the next!

GLOSSARY

afterlife (AF-tur-life)—the place where Egyptians believed a person's soul went after death

amulet (AM-yoo-let)—a small charm believed to protect the wearer from harm

bacteria (bak-TEER-ee-uh)—microscopic living organisms that can cause disease

canal (kuh-NAL)—a channel that is dug across land; canals join bodies of water so that ships can travel between them

draft (DRAFT)—the selection of young men to serve in the army

linen (LIN-uhn)—a cloth made from the flax plant

mummification (muh-mi-fuh-KAY-shun)—the process of making a mummy to preserve a dead person's body

nerve (NURV)—a bundle of thin fibers that sends messages between your brain and other parts of your body

quarry (KWOR-ee)—a place where people dig or cut stone from the ground

READ MORE

Adamson, Heather. *Ancient Egypt: An Interactive History Adventure*. You Choose Books. Mankato, Minn: Capstone Press, 2010.

Ganeri, Anita. *Ancient Egyptians*. Ancient Civilizations. Minneapolis: Compass Point Books, 2007.

Orr, Tamra. *How'd They Do That in Ancient Egypt?* How'd They Do That. Hockessin, Del.: Mitchell Lane Publishers, 2010.

INTERNET SITES

FactHound offers a safe, fun way to find Internet sites related to this book. All of the sites on FactHound have been researched by our staff.

Here's all you do:

Visit *www.facthound.com*

Type in this code: 9781429654067

Super-cool stuff!

Check out projects, games and lots more at
www.capstonekids.com

INDEX